The Classic

HARLEY-DAVIDSON

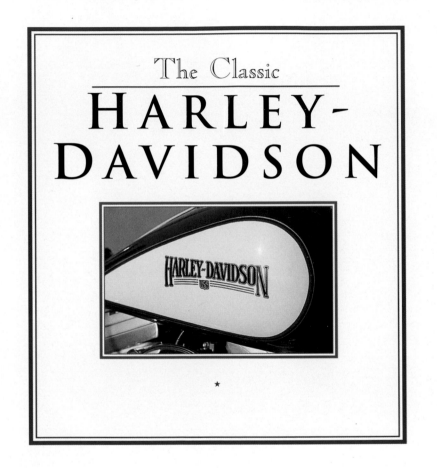

★

The Classic

HARLEY-DAVIDSON

A celebration of America's legendary motorcycles

★ ★ ★

Martin Norris

LORENZ BOOKS

This edition first published in 1997 by Lorenz Books
27 West 20th Street, New York, NY 10011

Lorenz Books are available for bulk purchase for sales promotion and for
premium use. For details, write or call the sales director:
Lorenz Books, 27 West 20th Street, New York, NY 10011; (800) 354-9657

Lorenz Books is an imprint of Anness Publishing Limited

ISBN 1 85967 504 2

Publisher: Joanna Lorenz
Project Editor: Fiona Eaton
Designer: Andrew Heath

Printed and bound in Singapore

3 5 7 9 10 8 6 4 2

CONTENTS

INTRODUCTION

The development of the Harley-Davidson motorcycle has, from its very beginning, been inextricably linked to the turbulent history of modern America. From the motorcycle's humble beginnings as a back garden experiment by the sons of immigrants, it has evolved into a universal symbol of freedom, and the most revered motorcycle in the world.

The Harley and Davidson families emigrated in the 1880s from Great Britain to America, where they were bound together by a friendship between two of their offspring, William (Bill) S. Harley and Arthur Davidson. The two childhood friends spent much of their spare time cycling and fishing together and, when old enough, both worked at the same metal fabricating plant in their home town of Milwaukee, Wisconsin.

At the end of the 19th century, competition cycling was a major sport in America and attracted large crowds to the indoor board tracks. This was where motorcycles were first seen in America in 1899, being used as pacers at a racing competition.

During the following year a work colleague showed Bill and Arthur a set of plans for the small De Dion type engine that powered these motorized bicycles. They experimented together, using the plans to build their own engines. Initially, they made several working models which,

Walter C. Davidson poses for a publicity shot after winning the 1908 FAM (Federation of American Motorcyclists) national endurance event with a perfect score. This two-day event in New York was the first of its kind in the country. The following week the FAM held an economy run in the city which Walter also won for Harley-Davidson, averaging 188 mpg.

according to some sources, were designed to power a boat for their fishing trips rather than a two-wheeled vehicle. But by 1901, they were concentrating their efforts on a motorized bicycle, and their first successful prototype took to the road in 1903. Its 405 cc (25 cu in) engine turned a leather loop that directly drove the rear wheel and powered the rudimentary machine at a brisk pace.

The quality of the first Harley-Davidson was markedly superior to the motorcycles then being sold by other amateur enthusiasts, and several people expressed an interest in purchasing one. Arthur's father erected a shed for the fledgling business in his backyard, and his aunt painted the legend on the door: "The Harley-Davidson Motor Co". With their own premises to work in and a growing confidence in their technical abilities, they began to capitalize on their small but growing reputation. A lack of money was a major problem for the duo but two deposits (each half the purchase of a motorcycle) enabled them to construct two more machines the following year, and double the size of their "factory" to 3 x 9 m (10 x 30 ft).

Bill and Arthur were not the only ones designing new motorcycles. Other young men in America were also selling the results of their backyard labour – as many as 300 different manufacturers. Most used the same approach, which was ultimately why most of them failed after selling only one or two machines. They just attached the engine to a bicycle without adapting it to cope with the stresses imposed by the engine. It did not take long before the rough and rutted roads of the day, and the absence of any suspension, exposed the weaknesses of this design, which could literally collapse under the rider. What made the Harley-Davidson superior to much of the competition was the more rugged construction of the frame and forks. Indeed, the common trait amongst all of the American motorcycle manufacturers who survived and grew out of these pioneering years was the attention paid to developing the whole machine. The reputation of Harley-Davidsons for being over-engineered, overweight and having larger engines than most motorcycles was born almost the moment the black paint on their second motorcycle had dried. In 1913, the company's advertisements boasted how this machine was still running, 100,000 miles and several owners later.

It was not just the high quality of their motorcycles that was responsible for their initial success, but the way they furthered their technical knowledge. Bill enrolled in an automotive engineering course while Arthur continued constructing their early motorcycles with the help of a few part-time employees. With such a positive and forward-thinking attitude, it is not surprising that the company grew at a rapid pace. Five years after their first motorcycle was sold their output had grown from one to 450 machines a year, and production had left the garden shed and moved into a small factory. They were also joined by two of Arthur's brothers, Walter and William, and this quartet controlled the business until they passed it on to the next generation.

1996 FLHTCUI. The Ultra Classic Electra Glide features almost everything a rider could want – CB radio, voice-activated intercom and music system – as well as maximum weather protection.

The motorcycle that brought them such success was the Silent Grey Fellow. Their first machines were painted black, but when grey became an option a couple of years later it rapidly became the preferred choice, and then the only colour available. Each year this motorcycle was improved with new technology, but its intrinsic qualities remained the same. The single-cylinder engine grew from 405 cc to 565 cc (25 to 35 cu in) and the machine offered quiet operation, subdued colour and dependability.

The largest Fellow was capable of 80 kph (50 mph) by the time a new and more powerful engine was developed, and then adopted, by nearly every motorcycle manufacturer in America, including Harley-Davidson. The motorcycle frames of the day had a lot of empty space behind the engine, and once the size of the single-cylinder had been optimized, the number of cylinders was increased to fill this gap. Attaching another cylinder to the existing engine meant that its capacity could be doubled with a minimal amount of extra weight and without requiring completely new design technology. Most American motorcycle manufacturers adopted the 1000 cc (61 cu in) V twin engine, and Harley-Davidson were not going to be an exception to such a practical innovation. The most notable characteristic of a V twin engine is that it is relatively slow-revving, and is consequently durable, generating a large amount of torque. These were ideal attributes for an American motorcycle that had to operate over long distances, often propelling a sidecar with passengers.

World War I, which began in Europe in 1914, caused a dip in the demand for, and total number of, motorcycles that were produced in America. But Harley-Davidson managed to sustain their rapid growth during the decade, while most of their competitors foundered and disappeared. Their export market may have been decimated and the cost of importing components may have risen, but domestic sales remained buoyant.

While this war hindered Harley-Davidson's world expansion plans it did enable them to topple their great rivals, Indian, as the largest motorcycle manufacturer in America. Indian had been one of the pioneers of American motorcycling and had remained at the forefront, selling more machines than any other company, but their fortunes now began to change. The military needed motorcycles and while Harley-Davidson offered half of their production to the government, Indian, believing that they were being more financially astute, turned over their entire production to supplying motorcycles to the army. By the time hostilities ended in 1918 many of Indian's dealerships, which had not been supplied with any motorcycles for two years, had switched allegiance to Harley-Davidson or closed down altogether.

Harley-Davidson had created their empire with just two models, the Silent Grey Fellow single, and the V twin, and by 1920 were the largest motorcycle company in the world. That year 28,189 motorcycles left the factory gates in Milwaukee, and were distributed and sold at their dealerships in 67 countries. However, during the early 1920s there was a post-war readjustment in the American economy that resulted in a huge drop in sales, not just for Harley-Davidson, whose output fell to 10,202 in 1921. Motorcycle sales were also being hit by the motor car industry, particularly by Ford, whose mass-production techniques meant that the cost of an automobile was now not much more than a top-of-the-range motorcycle. At the time Harley-Davidson's smallest

motorcycle was 1000 cc (61 cu in), but the company felt that there was a market for cheaper transportation. A 350 cc (21 cu in) single cylinder was produced but Americans could not be tempted, although it was a successful export and helped sustain the company during the 1920s. The 1000 cc (61 cu in) and 1200 cc (74 cu in) machines that Harley-Davidson produced may have been unwieldy for some riders, but a 350 cc (21 cu in) seemed too small. For many riders an American motorcycle had to be a large V twin.

A celebrated compromise appeared in 1929 with the launch of the 45. This 750 cc (45 cu in) V twin remained in production for 45 years, spending the last part of its life powering the three-wheeled Servi-Car. But no sooner had the company recovered after the problems of a decade before when the stock market crash of 1929 threatened to wipe them out completely. Indeed, with the exception of Indian, every other motorcycle company in the country went out of business by 1931. Harley-Davidson's production dropped from 22,350 to 3,703 within five years as the American economy collapsed. To make matters worse, the 45 and 1200 cc (74 cu in) model V that they had launched the following year both suffered from mechanical weaknesses which tainted their reputation until the models from this era were withdrawn and corrected.

There was tremendous post-war interest in motorcycling. With Indian motorcycles and their 1200 cc (74 cu in) Chief in limited production, the Knucklehead was king. Since the larger F and FL were only in limited production, the smaller versions of the Knucklehead are the most common.

Just when it seemed things could not get any worse, the company lost an important court case concerning a copyright infringement, and had to pay out $1.1 million. Harley-Davidson managed to struggle on by vigorously pursuing block sales to police and government departments, but once the technical faults were cured on the 45 and V their reputation revived.

Since World War I nearly every Harley-Davidson had worn a coat of green paint called olive drab that was the standard livery on their military machines. At first it was a fashionable colour, but 15 years later it had understandably become rather monotonous, as had the standard grey before. With the onset of the depression, however, Harley-Davidsons could suddenly be ordered in virtually any colour, and every year a new art deco design was applied to the petrol tank.

Up until 1936 Harley-Davidson had specialized in producing large capacity, side-valve motorcycles. These had some advantages over other engine designs, but were also rather slow in comparison to overhead-valve (OHV) engines. The 61E, which appeared that year, was the first OHV V twin they made and was a completely new direction for the company, both mechanically and stylistically. Its 1000 cc (61 cu in) OHV engine could produce 50 per cent more power than its model V predecessor, as was demonstrated when a highly tuned 61E set a new American speed record of 217 kph (136 mph). It was not long before the 61E became affectionately known as "The Knucklehead", for the shape of the rocker covers on top of the engine resembled the back of a fist. Its successors also came to be known by nicknames instead of their designated model numbers and letters; hence the Panhead from 1948 and Shovelhead from 1966, because the tops of their engines looked like upside-down baking pans and the backs of shovels!

After the 883 cc (55 cu in) Xl Sportster's debut in 1957 came a more awesome version, the XLCH. It was originally sold as a competition version with no lights or battery at the suggestion of a number of Harley-Davidson dealers, but became so sought-after that road-going versions were produced. The 1962 models were the fastest ones they made, producing a 14.3 second 0.25 mile (0.4 km) time and top speed of around 193 kph (120 mph), and were way ahead of the pack.

The introduction of the Knucklehead coincided with a trickle of British motorcycles that were imported into America in the mid-1930s. World War II understandably halted this trade, but just a few years after hostilities ceased more than a third of all new motorcycles sold in America were foreign. This was all the more galling for they were subjected to a very low import duty, while American motorcycles attracted up to 50 per cent duty when sold abroad. The 500 cc (30 cu in) OHV Triumphs and Nortons that were arriving in America were not only cheaper than Harley-Davidson's 45, but were good for an extra 32 kph (20 mph). For the time being though, the company chose to ignore this middle market and development was concentrated on their "big twins". Just prior to American involvement in World War II control of the company passed down to the next generation of the two families, as the sons of the founders were promoted to the top positions. One of their first projects together has, for many enthusiasts, become the quintessential Harley-Davidson. The 1948 Panhead improved and refined the sometimes trouble-some Knucklehead engine, correcting its overheating and lubrication problems.

At the other end of the scale Harley-Davidson introduced a 125 cc (7.6 cu in) two-stroke machine in 1947, competing against several English models of the same size. It offered cheap transportation in the lean period after the war. The two-stroke single cylinder motorcycle remained in the annual line-up in many different forms right up until 1978.

In the early 1950s Harley-Davidson should have been reaping the benefits of the nation's growing post-war confidence and the imminent demise of Indian motorcycles, their last remaining American competitor. Instead, the British were spoiling it for them, not only seizing the market for medium-sized machines but also sales from the Panhead. Harley-Davidson's response in 1952 was the model K, a 750 cc (45 cu in) machine which was supposed to repulse the invaders. The K came equipped with several firsts for the company including a hand clutch/foot shift just as the imported machines, and a sprung suspension at the rear with a swing arm. However, it was another side valve engine and woefully under-powered in comparison to the OHV engines of the foreign imports. Tuned versions of the K and an enlargement to 883 cc (55 cu in) helped to maintain sales at a respectable level, but mourners were few at the end of its short life. It was replaced by the Sportster in 1957, an 883 cc (55 cu in) OHV that could outrun the foreign pack.

As they had long been the only American motorcycle manufacturers in a fiercely patriotic country, Harley-Davidson sales should have been very healthy by the mid-1960s. However, they were now having to compete with the incursion of British and Japanese motorcycles. These were often cheaper, more reliable and sophisticated than Harley-Davidsons and unsurprisingly the company's share of the market shrank to a tiny amount – around 6 per cent – and two-thirds of those sales involved their lightweight machines.

To try to reclaim some of the ground lost, the Panhead was updated in 1966 after a 17-

The KH 1954-56. The larger capacity of the 883 cc (55 cu in) KH helped restore a degree of credibility to the model with its top speed of around 152 kph (95 mph) – 24 kph (15 mph) higher than the 750 cc (45 cu in) model K.

year run, becoming the 1200 cc (74 cu in) Shovelhead. This top-of-the-range model carried all the touring essentials that the Panhead had done before, but its weight had now swollen to 363 kg (800 lb), enough to ensure that it could barely reach 152 kph (95 mph). The bike was perfect for cruising at moderate speeds but many riders thought this tourer too big, dull and respectable, while Harley-Davidson's other V twin, the sleeker and faster Sportster, was just a bit too small.

Customizing motorcycles had been a growing phenomenon since the early 1960s, particularly on the west coast where shops had sprung up to cater for those enthusiasts. By taking a Panhead or Shovelhead and stripping off all of the excess weight and touring accessories, then adding a few radical parts, a rider could create a lighter, personalized machine that would perform more like a 1200 cc (74 cu in) motorcycle should. But Harley-Davidson refused to acknowledge or cater to this market, made up, they thought, of the more rebellious enthusiast. This aloofness undoubtedly contributed to the financial problems that eventually befell the company.

Harley-Davidson were selling motorcycles to a decreasing market and, with increased competition from imports, their fortunes dwindled. Going public and selling shares in 1965 offered a temporary respite to their financial problems as corporate predators began taking an interest. Four years later it became apparent that the only way for Harley-Davidson to survive was if control of the company passed out of their hands. After 66 years as a family business they were taken over by the American Machine and Foundry Company (AMF), better known for building bowling alleys. This takeover has come to be regarded by many enthusiasts as a dark period in the company's history.

As a leisure firm with a wide range of interests, AMF were not perceived as being at all interested in motorcycling, but they did invest substantially in Harley-Davidson's updating of production techniques, which made a significant difference within a short space of time. The AMF-led company also finally acknowledged that there was a huge demand for customized motorcycles, and grew less reticent about supplying what these enthusiasts wanted. In 1971 they produced the FX series, the first of several new models that contributed to a sales boost from 26,000 to 70,000 machines within five years. Unfortunately, quality control did not maintain the same pace and a reputation for unreliability began to taint their image. Harley-Davidson had always been a family business and their customers had been made to feel a part of it. But after the take-over the company was perceived as just another corporation, pedalling a product that they did not care about, to people whose money they were happy to take, but whose need they were not interested in.

A number of the founders' descendants still remained in senior positions after the take-over, but they found themselves increasingly marginalized and powerless. AMF then grew disenchanted with the motorcycle industry for though they made a profit, it was a minute amount compared to their other business earnings.

The Servi-Car was a popular choice for delivery companies and police departments, and was fitted with a reverse gear and three forward ones. The rear box was initially made of metal but during its final years was replaced by a glass-fibre unit.

During AMF's tenure, development began on a replacement for the Shovelhead, and tests were conducted on a water-cooled, four-cylinder V twin; an engine design that would run cooler, quieter and more efficiently than any previous Harley-Davidson. This was not likely to appeal to enthusiasts for whom a Harley-Davidson engine is a 45 degree, air-cooled V twin with two cylinders, just like the first V twin and every one since. Fortunately, another engine was developed in the late 1970s and the new owners understood precisely what their customers wanted. The V4 was shelved and an update of the Shovelhead was launched in 1984 to great acclaim. The 1340 cc (80 cu in) Evolution, so-called because it had evolved from the Shovelhead engine, is a complete anachronism in the modern motorcycle world today. Its engine bears many mechanical similarities to the Knucklehead which appeared half a century before, while many of the current models that it powers are deliberately styled to look equally old: a perfect blend of new technology and nostalgia.

Harley-Davidson have seemed almost backward-looking at times; often reluctant to take a progressive and bold leap forwards when a step sideways was possible. However, without this apparent conservatism, Harley-Davidsons would probably have evolved into motorcycles indistinguishable from their many soulless contemporaries. Today, it is apparent that they still retain their respect for the past, and have not forgotten about the sense of continuity and tradition that are the features of a family business. These magnificent machines, like their riders, celebrate the triumph of individual expression over monotonous conformity.

Eleven years after their optimistic take-over AMF wanted to quit the motorcycle industry, expecting another large conglomerate to take it off their hands. Instead, a number of executives from AMF Harley-Davidson, including the grandson of one of the founding brothers, Willie G. Davidson, offered to buy it back for $80 million. A consortium of banks backed them and, when the deal was done, the new owners reclaimed Harley-Davidson for its enthusiasts.

EARLY YEARS

The First Singles and V Twins

Bill Harley and the three Davidson brothers, William, Walter and Arthur, were not the only group of young men experimenting with motorcycles. The single-cylinder De Dion type engine was a simple design that worked so well that it was adapted by most of the fledgling motorcycle builders in the early 1900s. Harley-Davidson's first prototype based on this engine was just 167 cc (10 cu in), too small for any practical use, but the size of their second in 1903 was 405 cc (25 cu in), more than adequate for the day. It had a larger engine than most rival machines, setting a trend that still applies, and was in general better engineered.

Technical innovation and development moved at a rapid pace in those early years and the Silent Grey Fellow consistently set the standard for other manufacturers to follow. At the end of its life in 1918, the single-speed motorized bicycle had grown into a three-speed motorcycle capable of 80 kph (50 mph).

Harley-Davidson's second model, available in 1909, held a 45 degree V twin engine in its frame. Ever since its launch the company have always had a V twin motorcycle in their line-up, and so synonymous has it become with Harley-Davidson that today they make nothing but V twins. But the design of the final drive of this first engine did give problems and it was withdrawn after one year. Like the Single it had no tensioning device for the leather belt, but

This reproduction of the first Harley-Davidson shows how similar it was to a bicycle in style. Even its top speed of 40 kph (25 mph) had to be checked in the traditional way – by pedalling backwards.

while that was not a problem on the smaller motorcycle, the extra power of the V twin engine led to the belt slipping.

Re-introduced with a belt-tensioning device in 1911, it was better equipped to handle the 7 hp it produced and furthermore Harley-Davidson now had a motorcycle that was able to carry a sidecar. The following year the more practical chain drive became available, and was strong enough to cope with the power and displacement increase to 1000 cc (61 cu in) in 1914, and 1200 cc (74 cu in) in 1922.

The capacity and development of the "F head" engine reached its peak in 1929, when it was available with a magneto ignition like the 1000 cc (61 cu in) model F and 1200 cc (74 cu in) FD, or electrically equipped like the J and JD. It received one final boost for the last two years of its life. The much celebrated "Two Cammers", JH and JDH, used performance technology from the company's competition motorcycles. They may have been able to hit higher speeds than other motorcycles, but their temperamental reliability meant that they sometimes did not reach their destination.

Opposite: The last year of automatic inlet valves on all the Silent Grey Fellows was 1912. The following year mechanical inlet valves were fitted on the V twins, ushering in the era of the F head engine.

T h e S i l e n t G r e y F e l l o w

Above: *Apart from a small number of black motorcycles in the beginning and green ones towards the end of its life, grey was the only colour available for the Single (this is a 1912). The only choice to the customer was the colour of the pin-striping.*

Right: *The engine capacity of the Single eventually expanded to 565 cc (35 cu in) from its original 1903 size of 405 cc (25 cu in). This 1912 engine is a 494 cc (30.16 cu in) version, the stepping stone between the two.*

Opposite: *The 1912 Single was fitted with a clutch for the first time which was controlled by a second lever on the left, behind the larger belt tensioner. Once the pedals had fired up the engine, a smoother start was possible.*

The First V Twins

Above: *The 1928 JDH. The Two Cammer was a road-going JD that benefited from developments in racing engines. When set up correctly it could touch 160 kph (100 mph), which was faster than any other standard motorcycle. Unfortunately it was also prone to overheating, and breakdowns were par for the course.*

Above right: *The Two Cammer was a lean machine all round. It had narrower tanks, shorter handlebars, and wheels 5 cm (2 in) smaller than the more sedate JD.*

Right: *The JD (this is a 1925 example) was built to rival Indian's 1200 cc (74 cu in) Chief. With more torque, acceleration and speed than its 1000 cc (61 cu in) predecessor it was ideal for hauling a sidecar. This was a wonderful advantage for riders wanting to transport illegal liquor in a hurry during the prohibition years.*

Above: The final year that the 1000 cc (61 cu in) V twin was made with the square petrol tank was 1915. The three-speed transmission was introduced this year, operated by the lever on the left of the petrol tank.

Right: This unrestored V twin would probably fall in value if it even smelt a tin of polish. In Harley-Davidson's early years they did not always fully document the variety of striping and colours in which their grey bikes were finished. Original examples like this are invaluable to today's restorers.

Opposite: The 1914 V twin. The spark plugs were situated in the valve chambers or pockets of the F head, hence the term "pocket valves" was often applied to these engines.

SURVIVING THE DEPRESSION

The 45, Models V and U

The time came when the "F head" motors had to be replaced by a more technically advanced design, but rather than going for an overhead-valve engine, which was an increasingly popular design for foreign manufacturers, Harley-Davidson chose a side valve.

The first of these was the 45, Harley-Davidson's competitor to the Indian 101 Scout. But it was overweight and underpowered in comparison and needed to go through two changes – the models D (1928–31) and R (1932–36) – before it was at least as good. The latter 750 cc (45 cu in) eventually became the W in 1937 after receiving the recirculating oil system and stylistic changes brought in by the Knucklehead the previous year. The final year for the 45 was 1951, but the three-wheeled Servi-Car that appeared in 1932 remained on the factory books until 1974. The 45 was never a very powerful engine, and with the addition of the extra weight of the Servi-Car was not suited for recreational use. But as a utility vehicle that could run around town all day it was in its element.

Like the 45, the 1200 cc (74 cu in) model V suffered from mechanical problems when it went on sale in 1930, and production had to be halted until the faults were rectified. It certainly did not help that it was launched at the beginning of the depression as "the greatest achievement in motorcycle history",

The model V could produce slightly more power than the Two Cammer, but with a weight disadvantage of around 54 kg (120 lb) it was not really faster.

and for the remainder of its six-year run it never really overcame its reputation for being unreliable.

The model V may have been underdeveloped when it left the factory, but while on sale to the public its mechanical problems were sorted out. Like the 45, the model V was given many of the new Knucklehead features in 1937, and became the new model U. By that time all the engine's inherent faults had been rectified, and it became a very reliable machine.

It had been traditional to use side-valve engines in both American cars and motorcycles. These "flatheads" had a loyal following that helped sustain the company during the difficult years up to 1942. Shortly after the end of the war production of all the large side valves ended. The Knucklehead was becoming their most popular machine and it was not economically sensible to make two vastly different top-of-the-range machines in the post-war years.

Opposite: Around 88,000 military 45s were produced by Harley-Davidson, with enough spares to construct about 20 times as many machines again. At the end of the war many were sold off as surplus at bargain prices, or dumped when their service life ended. Consequently these machines turn up all over the world, and restoring a military 45 is not as daunting a prospect as it would be for a Model U or Panhead of similar age.

The 45

Above: *After its inauspicious debut in 1929, the 45 turned into a dependable workhorse that was the ideal utility motorcycle. This example was used as a breakdown support vehicle in Holland.*

Left: *This Military Police 45 carries a gun in the holster strapped to the front forks, and an ammo box on the other side.*

Opposite: *At a glance the 45 engine looks very similar to the larger side-valve engines, the models V and U. The most obvious difference between these models is that the final drive chain on the 45 is on the right-hand side of the motorcycle, while the larger machines have theirs on the left.*

The Model V

Above: *The 1934 model V tank featuring the teak red and black colour scheme, one of two standard colour options available that year.*

Left: *The 1936 model V. There were several changes introduced to the side valve in 1936 so that the new Knucklehead would not totally eclipse it. A four-speed gearbox and 1340 cc (80 cu in) engine were available for the first time, as were black wheel rims at no extra cost.*

The Model U

Above: *The model U did very well for Harley-Davidson. Sales to police forces were particularly important once the depression had set in and the competition with Indian for these lucrative fleet orders was fierce.*

Right: *The 1947 UL. According to Harley-Davidson, more man-hours were spent making one cylinder head for a side-valve engine than Chrysler needed to finish one six-cylinder block for an automobile.*

CLASSIC YEARS

The Knucklehead and Panhead

Harley-Davidson had produced a number of prototype and racing machines with overhead-valve engines but the side-valve design had fewer parts, was low maintenance and cheaper to produce. However, once their competitors had begun to sell overhead-valve motorcycles the company finally gave the go-ahead to their own project.

The 1936 Knucklehead introduced many new features to Harley-Davidson, and was their first modern motorcycle. The new OHV engine was supported on either side by a double-cradle frame instead of the single tube which was the last legacy of the motorcycle's bicycle ancestry. There was still no rear suspension on the frame, but the sprung post on which the seat was mounted still worked so well that it was not really necessary. The Knucklehead engine is directly related to today's Evolution, and it is a testament to its excellent design that many of the innovative features of this engine are still used on current Harley-Davidsons, more than 60 years later.

Not that much changed when the Panhead replaced the Knucklehead in 1948, apart from the new top end (barrels and cylinder heads), hydraulic lifters, and improvements to the oil system. The rest of the motorcycle was of sound construction, and remained much the same when it was re-christened. But every couple of years after the Panhead was introduced it received a major modification, with the result that it was a significantly different machine which bore the same nickname in 1965. The springer forks were replaced after only one year by hydraulic items, a foot shift/hand clutch option was offered from 1952, a new frame was substituted two years later, the bottom end was strengthened and the cases changed in 1955, a rear suspension was added for 1958, and an electric starter was added for its final year.

Above: The Knucklehead had two fuel tanks (the main tank, and the reserve) with the instrument panel sandwiched between them.

Opposite: The 1946 Knucklehead. From 1940 on, chrome name-plates replaced the painted art deco logos on the petrol tank. The style continued to change slightly every year.

The Knucklehead

Above: *The Knucklehead's new re-circulating oil system replaced the total-loss system of the earlier side valves. But soon after the launch there were numerous reports of very low oil mileage and oil leaks, both rectified the following year.*

Right: *The 1939 EL 1000 cc (61 cu in). The EL, the sportier of the 1000 cc (61 cu in) versions, was good for an honest 152 kph (95 mph), while its larger incarnation, the FL, could reach the magic ton.*

The Panhead

Above: *The 1965 Electra Glide. For its final year the Panhead came with an electric starter, powered by the huge battery under the seat. The extra weight of this new 12-volt system contributed to the bike's total curb weight of 355 kg (783 lb), almost 90 kg (200 lb) more than the Hydra-Glide.*

Right: *The 1948 Panhead. The Panhead had the traditional Springer front end fitted for the first year only, and was available in a vibrant azure blue.*

Opposite: *The 1964 Duo-Glide. This was the last year for the kick-start Panhead. Although it was not difficult to kick over, starting could be tricky if the motorcycle was not well maintained.*

Above: The 1959 Duo-Glide. The Harley-Davidson "big twin" finally received suspension at the rear in 1958 - hence the name "Duo". Plastic saddlebags were a more solid alternative to the traditional studded leather items.

Right: The 1953 Hydra-Glide. The 1000 cc (61 cu in) Panhead was phased out in 1951 as the difference in cost between it and the larger 1200 cc (74 cu in) version was minimal.

Left: The 1949 Panhead. The problems with oil circulation and leaks were never completely sorted out on the Knucklehead, and the Panhead was the solution. Fitting new cast iron barrels, aluminium heads and internal oil lines helped keep the oil inside, and made for a cooler running engine.

Below: The Hydra-Glide. Harley-Davidson began to name their motorcycles in 1949 when their first telescopic forks were used on a "big twin". The first model to be christened with a name and reference letter or number was the Hydra-Glide.

MIDDLEWEIGHTS

The Model K and Sportster

Many felt that Harley-Davidson had been caught unawares by the post-war influx of English motorcycles. The company's rushed response was the model K, in 1952, which was underpowered and inferior in almost every respect. The only real consolation was the engine's new unit construction, with the crankcase and gearbox together and no longer separate items.

According to official sources the model K was introduced after development ran out of time on a 60 degree 883 cc (55 cu in) V twin. It was meant to be only a temporary middleweight machine until a modern replacement was completed. But this did not happen for five years, and the K had to sustain interest for Harley-Davidson customers until 1957. It did help though that the model K was boosted from 750 cc (45 cu in) to 883 cc (55 cu in) in 1954, becoming the model KH, and that other sportier versions became available. Nonetheless, it remained a gap filler.

The 883 cc (55 cu in) XL Sportster was initially a model K converted to an overhead-valve engine. But just a year later any similarity between the two machines seemed inconceivable when the awesome XLCH appeared. This machine could stay ahead of almost any other motorcycle on the road, until 15 years later the British and Japanese manufacturers eventually caught up with it. In the traditional company way more power was found by enlarging the engine to 1000 cc (61 cu in). During the rest of the 1970s its popularity was maintained by offering slightly customized versions.

The Sportster remains in the company's line-up 40 years after its launch, but now with an Evolution engine. Based on the original Sportster, the new alloy engine arrived in 1986 and has proved as reliable as its larger sibling.

Above: The XR 1000 was a version of the Sportster that lasted for only two years, from 1983–84. This street legal machine was based on the XR-750 that was so successful in dirt track competition and, like the racer, carried a carburettor per cylinder on the right and its exhausts high up on the left.

Opposite: Elvis Presley did not only indulge in Cadillacs – this 1956 KH was one of several Harleys owned by him.

The Model K

Above: *The KH 1954-56. The model K introduced many new developments that were already established on British motorcycles. They included a clutch operated by the left hand with a right-foot gear change, swing arm and rear springs.*

Right: *The 750cc (45 cu in) KR Dirt track racer. The racing version of the K engine (the R stood for racer) looked like the road bike from the outside, but many internal parts bore no relation at all. The K was produced as a road-going model with some of the hot KR parts inside – the KK.*

Left: The KH 1954-56. Only 539 KH models were sold in its final year. The KHK was the more popular version but even that did not sell many more. By converting much of the unit construction engine to overhead valves in 1957, something good came of it.

Below: The 1956 KHK. Both the K and KH were underpowered for their size, but were substantially improved when versions of both engines included various parts that had been developed in the racing department – the KK and KHK.

The Sportster

Above: *XL Sportster. All modern Harley-Davidsons have a tremendous potential for tuning. This Sportster has had a performance kit fitted which replaces the ignition, cam, exhausts, carburettor and brakes, and incorporates cosmetic changes like the tank and seat which are based on the XR-750 race bike.*

Left: *The 1968 XLCH. The peanut tank was first introduced to the Sportster range via the XLCH. Instruments were mounted on the handlebars or in the top of the headlight to keep this lean machine as uncluttered as possible.*

Opposite: *The 1996 XL1200C. The new Sportster Custom and 1200S Sport are today's top-of-the-range Sportsters. The lowered suspension on the Custom gives the machine a more low-slung look, while the Sport version comes with more practical styling – uprated tyres, brakes and suspension.*

SPLIT PERSONALITY

The Shovelhead

To create the Shovelhead engine the company once again used the technique applied when the Panhead replaced the Knucklehead: they installed a new top end on to an existing engine. These new cylinder heads were still aluminium and had the oil lines on the outside like the later Panheads, but now rocker boxes replaced the rocker covers.

The 1966 Shovelhead was still a touring machine first and foremost, geared more for comfort and cruising than high speeds. But while the company spent the late 1960s refining the Shovelhead's touring capabilities, other people were stripping as much off it as they could.

After their initial reluctance, Harley-Davidson eventually listened to the riders who wanted a motorcycle that was not a heavy tourer or medium weight Sportster. The result was the FX series, which removed all the touring parts and mated what was left with the front of the Sportster – the F from the FL tourer and the X from the XL Sportster. This hybrid was so successful that it soon outsold the traditional top-of-the-range touring machine. Other factory customs followed which became even more radical and imitative of the extreme choppers that many enthusiasts were constructing.

Left: The first Shovelheads were modified versions of the Generator Panheads, the bottom of the engine remaining relatively unchanged during the transition. The change came in 1970 when the Generator was swapped for an alternator, and the timing case cover became cone-shaped. These later Alternator Shovelheads are also known as cone engines.

Opposite: Stripped of its windshield, top box and saddlebags, the FLH took on a whole new look.

Above: The 1971 FX Super Glide. This was Harley-Davidson's first motorcycle that was aimed at the custom enthusiast. By attaching the narrow Sportster front end to the Electra Glide frame and engine they created the perfect blend between the two models. This model is usually seen in a white paint scheme, while the fibreglass seat was not a popular option and was replaced by a conventional unit the following year.

Left: FX Super Glide. Federal laws began to influence the way Harley-Davidsons were constructed in the 1970s. In 1972 it became compulsory for the foot shift to be on the left-hand side, and turn signals had to be fitted the following year. Styling touches like the reflectors on the forks were also fitted across the range.

Below: 1976 FLH Electra Glide "Classic". An art deco style logo that had not been seen since the 1930s reappeared on the tanks of this year's model.

Above: The clear windshield, that was introduced on the Panhead, remained a popular option for the Shovelhead owner who did not want the full touring package of painted fibreglass windshield and saddlebag attachments.

Left: The Shovelhead engine was enlarged to 1340 cc (80 cu in) in 1978. An engine this large had not been seen in a Harley-Davidson for 30 years, since the model U had been phased out.

Opposite: To comply with the strict noise and emission regulations during the 1970s this huge air filter was fitted. The style of exhaust pipes regularly changed in this period and this Super Glide features a two-into-one system.

MODERN TIMES

The Evolution

The Evolution engine that took over from the Shovelhead in 1984 attracted more attention and new riders to Harley-Davidson than any previous model had done. Not only was it reliable and efficient, but it looked and sounded like the motorcycles of 50–60 years before.

The current range of Evolution models numbers around 12 – all with the same 1340 cc (80 cu in) engine. The major differences between them all lie in the frames and styling – the FL series are the touring machines, FXR/Ds are the sportier style of motorcycle, while the FXSs have their rear suspension hidden under the engine so that the rear of the frame looks rigid, the rest of the bike echoing the Knucklehead or early "Choppers".

Air-cooled V twin engines of this size were designed when noise and pollution controls were unknown, and it has been increasingly difficult for Harley-Davidson to meet them. However, the conversion to lead-free petrol, restricting the power output and strangling the exhaust note, have helped keep the machine within the current guidelines. Whatever follows the Evolution will probably have to be a water-cooled engine, perhaps like one of the many current Japanese imitations. It does not bear thinking about.

Right: 1996 FLHRI Road King. This is the mid-way model between the Softail and Dyna Glide cruisers and the all-out tourers. The windshield and saddlebags can be swiftly removed and give this machine a dual personality. Like many of the top-of-the-range models it has an electronic fuel-injection system.

Opposite: FLSTN. Every modern Harley-Davidson is named by the company. This is the "Nostalgia", a limited edition of the "Heritage Softail" model, distinguished by stylistic changes such as the white wall tyres, shotgun exhausts and cowhide inserts in the seat and saddlebags.

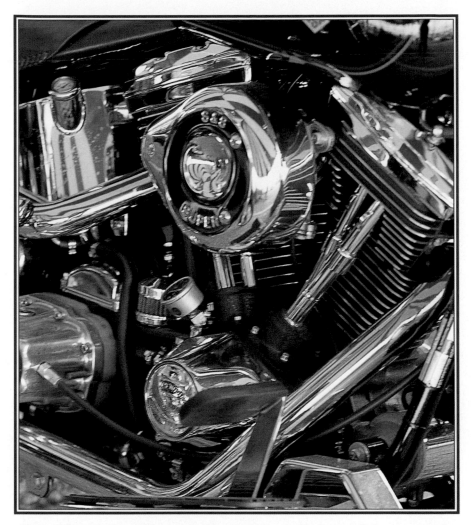

Above: *The 1340 cc (80 cu in) V2 engine is at the heart of the success that Harley-Davidson enjoys today. Introduced in 1984, it has proved oil-tight and reliable, yet remains similar to the Knucklehead on which it is loosely based.*

Left: *The owner of this Springer Softail has sensitively personalized it with new fenders, exhausts, paintwork, lights, etc. Compare the front of this motorcycle to that of the 1948 Panhead to see how little it has changed in 50 years.*

Above: 1996 FXDWG Dyna Wide Glide. Apehanger handlebars, wide forks and feet-forward controls give this model a respectable "chopper" style. The Dyna has a rubber-mounted engine to keep the vibration away from the rider, and a hidden balance pipe on the two exhausts.

Right: FXRT/P. The introduction of the Evolution engine enticed many police forces away from their foreign motorcycles and back on to Harley-Davidsons. The FXRT/P (P for police) is also available to the public, though you had better cover up the coloured lights and disconnect the siren before taking to the road.

Below: 1989 FXSTC Springer. The Knuckle, Pan and Shovel nicknames have been previously applied to "big twins" to describe the engine's cylinders. "Blockhead" never stuck when people were searching for a word to describe the cylinder heads on this engine, and everyone has now settled for the company's name – the Evolution.

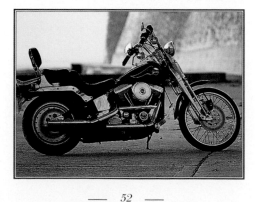

RACING

Harley-Davidson V twins have always enjoyed extensive racing success in America, but only a limited amount on the world's circuits.

During their early days the company made limited numbers of special racing machines that were offered to selected riders, and they also had a celebrated racing team until 1921 called "The Wrecking Crew", which was disbanded after repeatedly trouncing the opposition. It was not until the introduction, in 1934, of Class C racing for production motorcycles and serious amateurs that interest in competition was revived. It had become more affordable for manufacturers to get involved in racing again, and consequently the class was taken over by professional riders on Harley-Davidson and Indian factory-prepared machines. At first the W model 45 was pitted against the Indian Scout, but after the war the model K's main rivals were British motorcycles.

While the road-going version of the model K expired in 1956, the rules of Class C racing so suited Harley-Davidson that they had no need to develop a new motorcycle until 1969. When the rules were changed to allow any machine up to 750 cc (45 cu in) to enter, the XR-750 was introduced to compete against the new Triumphs and BSAs. Harley-Davidsons were never really suited to road racing, and when the multi-cylinder Japanese machines came along in the early 1970s they stuck to the dirt tracks where they still had the edge.

Recently Harley-Davidson have begun racing with a completely new motorcycle, the VR 1000. Racing success with this machine might well inaugurate a road-going model that would help the company make the transition to selling water-cooled motorcycles. However, the VR has frequently broken down in competition and has not achieved the expected results.

Above: *The VR 1000 signalled Harley-Davidson's entrance into Superbike racing at the end of the 1980s. The water-cooled, 60 degree, V twin with four valves per cylinder is unlike any other Harley-Davidson, but has not yet been a great competition success.*

Opposite: *When the racing K model was introduced in 1952 it had to be a very versatile machine. It needed a rigid frame for the oval dirt tracks – the KR – and rear suspension and drum brakes for road and TT courses – the KRTT. The national racing series in the 1950s required rider and machine to compete on 1.6 km (1 mile), 0.8 km (1/2-mile), and 0.4 km (1/4-mile) ovals, dirt circuits with jumps, and road circuits. These 750 cc (45 cu in) side valves competed against 500 cc (30.5 cu in) overhead-valve British motorcycles according to the rules, consistently winning until they were changed in 1969 allowing any 750 cc (45 cu in) machine to compete.*

Above: The XR-750 was a rushed solution to a change in racing rules for the 1969 season. Harley-Davidson needed a competitive 750 cc (45 cu in) machine in a hurry, so they took the 883 cc (55 cu in) Sportster and de-stroked it to the required size. In typical Harley-Davidson fashion, the machine was very uncompetitive for the first couple of seasons, but it then went to the front of the pack and for 15 years consistently beat the opposition on dirt tracks.

Left: The engine in the racing model K was never the best in the field, but the KR and KRTT won the national championship for 12 of the 17 years that it competed. This was a tribute to tuners of the day such as Tom Sifton, who could always extract a bit more power when it was needed.

Opposite: In the pursuit of power, a large engine is a good starting point. Harley-Davidsons are a popular choice for drag racing though many, if not most, of the components on these machines come from specialist accessory manufacturers.

CUSTOMIZING

Customizing is almost as old as motorcycling itself. In the early days riders often had to modify their machines as many were mechanically primitive, and spares difficult to obtain. Harley-Davidson were a notable exception to the poor standard of construction of many early motorcycles, and they also encouraged their riders to purchase decorative accessories.

Motorcycle clubs were respectable social organisations in the 1920s and 30s, and customizing was generally limited to adding the company's approved extras to already overloaded touring machines. This changed after the war when a Californian style called the "Bobber" became popular, and riders started doing the complete opposite. Stripping the motorcycle of all the overweight touring accessories, and cutting back the heavier items like the large rear fender (shortened and bobbed like a dog's tail, hence the name "Bobber"), helped increase performance; it also made the motorcycle and rider look excitingly dangerous. This style was captured in the 1953 film *The Wild One*, which publicized it more widely, as did other movies in the mid-60s until *Easy Rider* gave the world the "Chopper", a more extreme and decorative Bobber style.

With the introduction of the Evolution engine, and the many new riders from all walks of life that flocked to Harley-Davidson, the custom has finally killed the idea that only society's outlaws modify their motorcycles.

Left: The Bay Area style came out of the 1970s as customs became lower following the extremes of the 1960s. The Sportster engine with its fast acceleration and sleek lines was perfect for a street racer like this. Subtlety has never been a primary concern of customizers, as this gold-plated engine shows.

Right: Recent years have seen a trend for full-fendered bikes, but the covering up has not stopped here and many customized bikes now leave little more than the engine exposed.

Boardwalk Classic
Bike Show

Above: New paint techniques have revolutionized the style and type of finish that can be applied to a customized bike, but morbid motifs remain perennially popular.

Right: While the Chopper had been seen in various exploitation films during the mid-1960s, Easy Rider (1969, starring Peter Fonda) propelled its image around the world. As a result Harley-Davidson had to produce their own highly sanitized customized bikes in the '70s to meet the demand. These faithful recreations of the bikes in the film were typical of what was then being done with Panhead engines.

Above: *Recent years have seen the development of paint that can withstand high temperatures. Now engine decoration is not limited to a choice of a few metal finishes and can, if desired, complement the style of most machines.*

Left: *Customizing usually begins with a vision, or occasionally, a strange dream. The beauty of the process is that each one is unique, and is not necessarily built to appeal to anyone but the owner.*

Above: *This modern custom has been built in the style of the early "bobbers", with its skinny front wheel, no mudguard, raised handlebars, Panhead engine and springer forks. It is owned by a member of "The Hamsters", a club whose membership includes most of the finest customizers in the world.*

Left: *Customizing is all about individual expression; ask Junky Jim who appears at most major events in the American motorcycling calendar. His machine has developed over the years with whatever he finds on the way.*

Opposite: *This machine takes its inspiration from the past. Built by an American accessory company, Milwaukee Iron, its Shovelhead engine powers a motorcycle that looks like an early racing machine.*

The 1947 WL. This 45 has high compression cylinder heads fitted to give an hp boost of 15 per cent.

1996 FLSTF Fat Boy. The solid wheels are for cosmetic reasons, and serve no practical purpose except to make them easier to clean. Some owners claim that they make this Evolution model difficult to handle in strong cross winds.